The story of the Arabic Bible ..

American Bible Society

THE STORY OF THE ARABIC BIBLE

A CARAVAN IN SYRIA

AMERICAN BIBLE SOCIETY
NEW YORK
1906

THE story of the Arabic Bible deals with a struggle begun by the fathers and bequeathed in trust to this generation—the struggle to domesticate the gospel of Jesus Christ in that wonderful language which Mohammedanism calls divine, and with which it has superseded Christian language, in Syria, Mesopotamia, and Egypt. The story begins with the Arabic alphabet and the than who shaped the type with which to print it.

The mission of the American Board had no sooner brought its printing press from Malta to Beirut in 1834, than Mohammedans criticized its Arabic type. The type had been made in Europe, and looked—well, about as English type would look if designed by an Arab. The Rev. Eli Smith saw that in plans for using the printing press as a teacher of the gospel, the quality of the equipment counts ; the press would be handicapped unless its type pleased the fastidious, artistic taste of Mohammedans. Such type did not exist ; therefore it was a duty to create it. He collected specimens of choice Arabic manuscripts and of writing-masters' beautiful models, and with a reed pen copied from them the letters of the alphabet to serve as models for the type. Since the letters of Arabic words are generally joined together in printing as in writing, each letter changes its form to suit its position ; and including the vowel points, about 1,800 different types are necessary to print one complete alphabet.

The preparation of these written models having been finished, Dr. Smith, in 1836, took passage in a little Prussian schooner for Smyrna, to watch over the cutting of the steel punches with which to strike the matrices used in casting type. The voyage ended in shipwreck, and all Dr. Smith's written models were lost under the smiling waters of the Mediterranean Sea.

Catastrophe is a spur to a determined man, and Dr. Smith at once began again at the beginning. He collected more specimens of fine writing and made a new set of models. Then Mr. Hallock, the American Board's printer at Smyrna, under Dr. Smith's guidance, skillfully cut the steel punches and struck the matrices.

[REV. ELI SMITH, D.D.

Providing types to print an alphabet may seem a very small thing, yet if there had been the slightest slip or change of form in designing the letters, or in cutting the steel punches, Mohammedans would have refused to read any book printed with that type. To this day book lovers among them prefer manuscripts to printed books. But this undertaking was so carefully and sympathetically carried out that when the work was done, the slant and curve of the letters and the thickness and swell of the lines were singularly perfect, according to the most critical Arab calligrapher's taste. So Smyrna, home of the second of the Seven Churches of Asia, had this added to the riches of its history: that it was closely connected with executing the plan of presenting the Christian Scriptures in the great Mohammedan language.

With the finishing of the matrices, a part only of the work was done. The whole batch of precious bits of

4

the ...
... in ...
... ...
... ...ously worked out in fine detail, ...
s...ful execution of the first part of a plan for a missionary literature campaign of the greatest importance.

The Scriptures had been translated into Arabic long
before this. The four Gospels, at least, were translated
in the sixth century. About the year 750 the Roman
Catholic Bishop of Seville translated the New Testament
and a part of the Old, for the benefit of the Moors of
Andalusia. In 1671 the Maronite Bishop Serkis issued
a translation of the Bible from the Vulgate; but it was
too costly to be any poor man's possession, it was inaccu-
rate, and its style was uneven. The British and Foreign
Bible Society, soon after its organization, adopted this
version and circulated it rather extensively in Syria and
Egypt. This was the version used for thirty years by
the American missionaries in Syria; but Mohammedans
reviled it, saying that the coarse diction and the graceless
form of the printed letters clearly proved the book to be
a shabby production of human enterprise, not at all in-
spired of God. Then in 1851 the Society for the Promo-
tion of Christian Knowledge (London) published an
Arabic version of the Scriptures made by Professor Lee
and Faris-es-Shidiak, an eminent Syrian writer; but
this version followed closely the King James' English
version, even reproducing its errors. The success of
missionary work in Syria, Egypt, and Arabia depended
upon the production of a new version which should
accurately render the original in perfect Arabic form.

s
ti
took th   se   ng
1841 it m   ri
Dr. Smith's beautiful new type, and it h
a specimen of this edition inscribed in Dr
handwriting.   In 1843 it furnished the money for a
tion of the Proverbs.

So, in 1848, when the Syrian Mission came to the Bible
Society with a request for $500 to pay for the support of a
native assistant to Dr. Smith in his work of translation,
the Society did not hesitate about participating in this
great enterprise.   Was it not in some degree a steward
of the Oracles of God ?   It made the grant, repeating it
in successive years, besides bearing the expense of printing the portions of the Bible as they were completed.
The Society from the very outset thus committed itself
to the financing of the enterprise.   Neither the Society
nor the generous donors of the money can ever regret
their share in the sacrifices which made the Standard
Arabic version an accomplished fact.

Dr. Smith's method of working was marked with the
thoroughness that characterized all of his undertakings.
The duty of his assistant, Mr. Bistani, was to prepare the
first draft of the translation, using the Syriac version as

6

ARAB VILLAGER AND HIS CAMEL

p[...]
un[...]
his [...] ha[...]
bade the p[...]
tran[...]ation. Exc[...]
the first t[...]lve cha[...]ers of [...] the rest [...]
be regarded as unfinished work. S[...] fell asleep, in the
place of his labors, on Sunday morning, January 11,
1857.

We commonly speak of the Arabic Bible as having
required sixteen years for its preparation, but Dr. Smith's
work from 1836 onward was definitely and closely re-
lated to the translation. He never relaxed for a moment
the study of the Arabic language. Since he steadily
labored on his preparations from that year, it is perfectly
proper to say that the translation of the existing Arabic
Bible cost the two great men, Smith and Van Dyck,
twenty-eight years of hard labor.

For a moment Dr. Smith's death seemed to crush
beyond reconstruction the enterprise of Arabic Bible
translation. The American Bible Society had spent
some $10,000 upon Arabic Scriptures, and had nothing to

show for this great outlay but a few volumes of an unsatisfactory, old version and piles of unfinished manuscript.

But one of the notable characteristics of the Bible enterprise in foreign mission fields is that those engaged in it have no faculty for perceiving defeat. The death

REV. C. V. A. VAN DYCK, D.D.

of the leader in this Bible translation meant, not stoppage of the work, but prompt action to find a new leader, also able to use Arabic as his own language. The Rev. Cornelius Van Dyck had been in the service of the American Board in Syria seventeen years at the time of Dr. Smith's death. He was one of the choice scholars of lation to a [...] printing of t[...] [...] 1865. This e[...] [...] Dr. [...] American Board, [...] characterized as "of [...] importance to a large portion of the human race," [...] appropriately celebrated by the missionaries. In the room where Dr. Smith had labored on the translation eight years, and Dr. Van Dyck eight years more, the missionaries assembled to pray and to thank God for the completion of the great undertaking. Then the sound of many voices arose from below, and a large company of young Syrians, workmen at the press and members of the Protestant community of Beirut, began to sing a hymn composed by one of their number for the glad occasion. The hymn was afterward translated from Arabic by the Rev. H. H. Jessup, D. D., as follows :

> " Hail, day thrice blessed of our God !
> Rejoice, let all men bear a part,
> Complete at length thy printed word,
> Lord, print its truths on every heart.

ags then to his Great Name."

In 18** the Rev. S. H. Calhoun, the Agent of the American Bible Society for the Levant, wrote, in a plea for funds for translation work : "Is it a matter of no interest or consequence to American Christians whether the people for whom these translations are intended have or do not have the Word of God in a language which they can understand? Oh, that Christians in America would reflect a little upon the condition of a nation which has no Bible !" Perhaps such language may help us to-day to understand the spontaneous outburst of joy which celebrated the completion of the Arabic version. "Surely not for many centuries," wrote one of the missionaries at Beirut, " have angels in heaven heard a sweeter sound arising from Syria than the voices of that band of young men ascribing glory and praise to God that now for the first time the word of God is given to their nation and tongue in its purity." Dr. Van Dyck, on finishing the translation, expressed his deep feeling in the midst of the general joy by sending fifty dollars to the American Bible Society as a thank-offering because he had been permitted to finish a work of paramount significance to the human race.

As soon as the translation of the Bible approached completion, the Syrian Mission, in March, 1864, had called upon the American Bible Society to electrotype it

11

i... ... ... Bible. As the printing p... been almost all purchased by the tions must be printed immediately. ... ...re consideration of the whole question, the Bible Society decided to grant the request of the Syrian Mission. The work was begun in 1866 as a special feature of the fiftieth year of the Society's existence, new Arabic type being cast in New York for the purpose. It was a memorable undertaking, destined beneficently to affect almost every non-Christian land.

The expenditure of the American Bible Society upon issues of Arabic Scriptures during seventy-six years probably exceeds $100,000. Since the new Standard Arabic version began to be printed in 1860, the Mission Press at Beirut (since 1870 being connected with the Presbyterian Board of Foreign Missions) had printed 1,076,518 volumes of Scripture in Arabic. It is sometimes not understood by casual observers that this is a work of the American Bible Society. Mr. Freyer, the superintendent of the Beirut Mission Press, writing for publication in April, 1904, felt it necessary to call attention to this fact. He says: "At the time of translation, the Bible in various sizes was set in type and electro-

MEMORIAL TABLET IN ARABIC IN THE ROOM
WHERE THE ARABIC BIBLE WAS
TRANSLATED

with [text obscured]
tributes, a [text obscured]
ceives at cost [text obscured]

The friends who have [text obscured] in previous years, and those who ha[ve] [text obscured] prevent its suspension in this year (1906), will nat[urally] [a]sk, before we leave this story of the Arabic Bible, "What is the good of it all ? What has been the result ?" The Book has gone forth from the Mission Press at Beirut into Syria, Mesopotamia, Arabia, and Egypt in many great editions ; the issues for 1905 somewhat exceeding thirty thousand volumes. It has been circulated in less degree among the teeming millions of all North Africa, from the Red Sea to the Atlantic Ocean. It has found its way across the Sahara to Timbuktu, and into the Mohammedan regions of north central Africa as far south as the Niger River on the west of the continent, and to Mombasa on the east. A regular demand for it exists at the Cape of Good Hope. It circulates to some extent among Mohammedans in Persia, Central Asia, India, China, and Malaysia. The Arabic Bible from Beirut has found readers in the Philippine Islands, in Yucatan, and in Brazil. The Syrian colonies in New York and in Chicago, as well as in Buenos Ayres, use this Bible, imported from Beirut for their benefit. The Syrian Mission has

14

are gi... ... verities taking fa... hold o... ...e
on of myriads, which no man can number, of the
...t and all future generations."

The fathers bore the burden of great toil and expenditure in providing the Arabic Bible ; the children inherit the duty of using it aright. It is not for any uncertain work or tentative enterprise that the American Bible Society asks the interest and the prayers of its supporters. The Arabic version is a proved success. It is one of the noblest of all versions in non-Christian languages, and the gospel is now at home in the language of Islam. All that we now have to do is to protect the text from printer's error and to see that supplies for printing and circulating this doubly sacred book are yearly made good. The increase of its circulation is a duty left to us in implicit trust by the heroes now entered into their rest. As was pointed out in an address of Bible Day, 1904, by the Rev. Dr. Hoskins of the Syrian Mission: "Not one of the original circle of workers of 1844 is left to speak to us to-day. Bright boys who entered the Press in those early days grew slowly into gray-haired men as they handled the millions of types necessary for each of the complete editions of the Bible. Some sacrificed the light of their eyes, others the cunning and skill of their hands, and then they passed out silently into the night of death. Eli Smith and Cornelius Van Allen Van Dyck gave their life-blood to the task. . . . Their memory, the fruits of their toil, we must hold as a secret trust. If we can toil

15

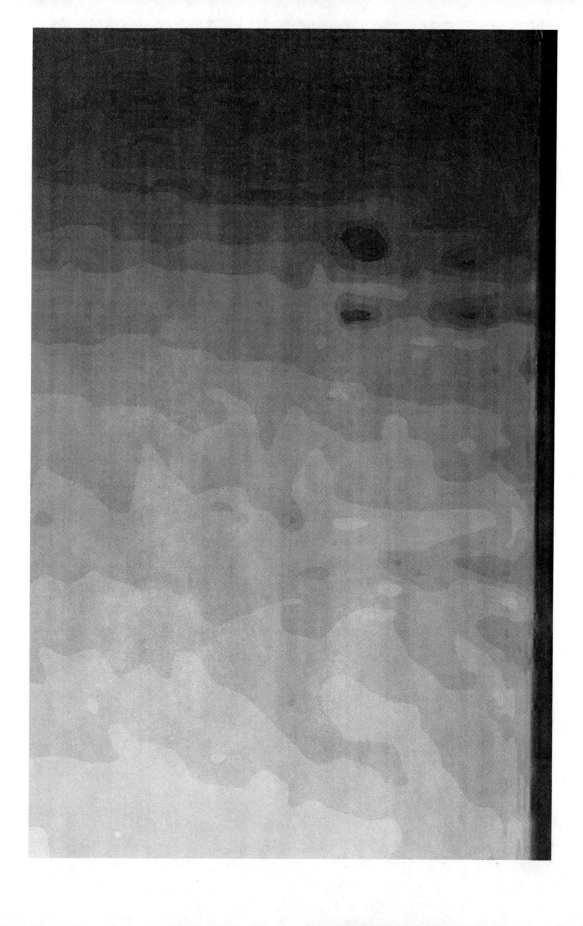

DATE DUE

JUN 1 ~ 1992			
JUN 1 7 1993			

CPSIA information can be obtained at www.ICGtesting.com
Printed in the USA
BVOW06s1909010814

361372BV00004B/9/P